ELLIE HAINES

Mental Stimulation & Fun Ideas For Dogs

Copyright © 2020 by Ellie Haines

All rights reserved. No part of this publication may be reproduced, stored or transmitted in any form or by any means, electronic, mechanical, photocopying, recording, scanning, or otherwise without written permission from the publisher. It is illegal to copy this book, post it to a website, or distribute it by any other means without permission.

First edition

Proofreading and editing by Chris Alibone & Diane Self
Special thanks to Jenna Tomlin, Jenny Youdan & Lisa Edwards

In loving memory of our mascot Busby xx

This book was professionally typeset on Reedsy.
Find out more at reedsy.com

Foreword

Walking
Feeding
Training
Tricks
Social Time
Car Journeys
Massages
Free Work
Grooming & Handling
Recycling

Useful Links
Recommended Reading
Notes

Foreword

Mackeson *Pudgey*

In September 2009, inspired by my boys Mackeson (Chocolate Labrador) and Pudgey (Springer Spaniel) I created Haines Hounds (HH). My aim was and still is to help owners to understand their dogs' specific requirements, leading to a more enjoyable life for everyone. I have since fostered and re-homed many dogs from a variety of backgrounds alongside running the business. I am now owned by Bosun, an adventurous Mastiff x Staffie and Riv, a very soppy Dobermann x German Shepherd.

HH has become hugely successful not only in its dog training and behaviour capacity but also in providing dog walking, sitting and boarding to the highest standards. I am so proud of our team and what we have achieved. Dogs are our passion. Learning as much as we can from them and other like-minded dog professionals is what we do best along with passing on what we learn onto our clients.

Since learning how beneficial mental stimulation can be for confidence building, exercising brains, and growing relationships I have been keen to inspire other dog lovers and provide tips and encouragement to explore a more fulfilling and enriching life for their dog - or their customers dogs' if that is the case. So let's dive in!!

Walking

It's easy to get caught in the trap of walking your dog in the same place every day, and taking the same routes, particularly if they are "safe" walks that you know and feel comfortable doing. However, walks are much more enriching and enjoyable for dogs when they get to explore things and go on new adventures.

As humans, we understand and investigate our environment through our sense of sight, whereas dogs predominantly use their sense of smell.

Allowing them to walk alongside bushes, tree lines, river banks and along the edges of fields helps to keep their noses entertained. It can also make your walk longer and more enjoyable as you will most likely be off the beaten track.

Peanut & Sammy exploring with Adam

Make a change to your walks, and go somewhere different!

Dogs really benefit from investigating new smells, finding new routes and learning about new environments. When dogs are sniffing, they cannot always hear you call them. Wait for their nose to come up before recalling, this will give you a much higher success rate!

Sammi loves investigating smells at the woods

Think about how different textures trap smells; grass, sand, bark, water, leaves and mud all hold onto smells for varying lengths of time. Follow your dog's nose and you too can enjoy a calmer, more relaxing walk.

Teach yourself to stand still when your dog sniffs!! Even when they are off the lead, learn to be very patient. The distance you cover is nowhere near as important as the sensory enrichment your dog is getting from their walk.

Bosun snuffling random tyres and sand piles

If you have access to a vehicle that is great as you can explore many new places with completely new smells. However, not to worry if you don't have access to a vehicle or if your dog is uncomfortable with traveling. You can pick a completely different route to your usual walk from the house - or to really allow your dog maximum enjoyment on their walk, let them lead the way!!

Dexter exploring the texture and smells of a fallen tree

Newton & Darwin prefer to sniff in longer grass

HH Hint: Dog leads are often too short which may be a factor in why some dogs tend to pull on their leads. Using a longer lead allows your dog to explore without having to pull in order to move. As you can see in the photos, our preferred walking equipment is a Y-Front fitting harness with (at least) a 2 metre lead attached to the back of the harness.

Bosun occasionally chooses to carry a toy on his walks
Chewing is an excitement reliever for dogs which can help to keep them calm

Feeding

Some dogs appear to inhale their food which means they eat a whole meal within just a few seconds. Others are seemingly very fussy, and will walk away from their bowl of food after sniffing at it or picking from it for a few seconds. Either way, mealtimes are often quite short-lived and are not that entertaining.

Spread out the daily food allowance to make mealtimes more interesting and give the filled enrichment toys throughout the day instead of feeding at set times

Being creative with your dog's food will provide them with much more enjoyable mealtimes, keep them entertained longer and can be calming for them too.

If your dog is fed on dry food you have multiple options for making their meals more enriching; you can put the dry food into treat balls, Kong Wobblers, Buster Cubes, SnuffleMats, and interactive toys such as Memory Trainers.

Riv loves a snuffle mat in the morning

Alternatively, you can soak the dry food and pack it into Kongs, Snack Snakes, and Busy Buddy Squirrel Dudes. There are many options available, lots of which can be found online and in the Pound shops.

Ben & Mollie enjoying their Scatter Feeding breakfast on the garden

If your dog is fed on wet food or raw minces you can smear these onto Licky Mats, or pack them into toys, you can even freeze their Licky Mats and toys for longer lasting enrichment.

Did you know that both licking and sniffing are self-soothing, meaning they have a relaxing effect on your dog's body and brain?

Simba loves frozen mince spread onto his slow feeder

You can also split wet or raw food minces into multiple small tubs, lids or paper plates and place them randomly around the house and garden for your dog to find.

Prepared enrichment toys in the freezer

Be sure not to make the games too difficult to begin with as they may become frustrating rather than enjoyable. Always supervise your dog during their first few attempts with enrichment toys to ensure they do not become frustrated, or try to eat the toy afterwards!

Belle nudging her dinner treats balls around the living room

The very reason we have dogs in our lives today is because historically, they were expert scavengers and hunters. Scavenging and hunting for food comes naturally to many dogs and giving them an outlet for this instinctive behaviour can be very rewarding.

Pepper finding hidden treats from under garden pots

HH Hint: If you have multiple dogs they may appreciate being separated to eat their food in peace, this will also help to prevent your other dog(s) trying to "help".

Pudgey experimenting with mashed banana and greek yogurt in his new toys

Training

Dogs are incredibly clever, they can learn hundreds of different cue words and hand signals. Many of the dogs we have in our lives today have a strong working heritage, they really enjoy learning new things and having their brains challenged.

Dogs do not generalise very well, which means in order to get the best, strongest and fastest responses from your dog, teach them their cues/hand signals in every location and situation in which you would like them to respond.

Charlie working on his self control with food and passing distractions

Build up your training slowly inside, outside, in pubs/cafes, in friends' houses/gardens and even in the vets waiting room.

Use your daily walks for training around distractions at a distance your dog is comfortable with.

Bailey working on her 'Down-Stay' outside

Chirag Patel's 'The Counting Game' is brilliant for training your dog outside, it is particularly useful for work with distractions.

Riv's recalls are really strong with 'The Counting Game' - she loves it!

Training should be fun and mutually enjoyable for both you and your dog. Use a pleasant tone and relaxed manner when training your dog and be flexible within your training sessions to allow for your own dog's abilities and preferences. Allow comfort to take priority over position. Alter your training cues to make it possible for your dog to still enjoy participating in training sessions.

Kiba Mackeson & Bosun working on 'Watch-Me' around distractions
Notice the different position of each dog

Dogs have four legs, which naturally makes their walking pace faster than ours. Having a 2 metre lead attached to a Y-Front Harness allows 'loose lead walking' easier to teach and becomes more natural and easier for dogs to maintain.

Teaching your dog how to walk on a loose lead is beneficial for both ends of the lead

HH Hint: If you're concerned about your dog putting on weight, you can use your dog's daily food allowance for rewards. Increasing the value of the treat from low end (daily food) to high end (ham, turkey, beef, liver etc.) when training outside in the big wide world can really help to motivate your dog around the multiple distractions out there.

Smaller treats allow for more enrichment fun - cut them up!

Tricks

Trick training is so much fun! There are so many variables to each trick, making them easier or harder, which means that tricks can be taught to any dog of any age or ability.

Pippa practising her "Spider" trick

Teach your dog cue words for each behaviour and a hand signal, practice both the cue word and hand signal separately so your dog now has two cues (a visual and verbal) for the same behaviour.

You can teach your dog something new, for example targeting objects and body parts. Targeting means teaching your dog to touch a location with their nose, paw, shoulder or hip. This can be an extremely useful trick that can lead to shutting doors, pushing buttons and even holding a very still position for examination purposes.

*Barkley targeting a knee
with his paw during a walk*

Alternatively, you could build on something that they already have an existing understanding of, for example if your dog understands how to sit, teach a sit-pretty, holding something whilst they sit, or to sit from a distance.

*Kiba learning the early stages of the
Cop-Cop trick (walking on my feet)*

Test your dog's understanding of cue words by practising them around distractions when outdoors, or by facing the wall/turning your back before asking them to show you a behaviour indoors.

Pudgey practising his "Middle" on the beach

Dogs have a 2 - 4 minute optimum attention span, use this to your advantage by setting up multiple mini training sessions throughout the day.

If you are unsure about how to teach a trick, or how to add further steps to an existing trick, there are many online tutorial videos that can help show you the steps!

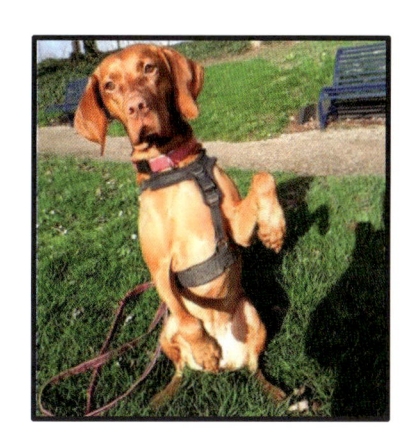

Pippa practising her "Beg" on a walk

Weigh your dogs daily food allowance and treats

HH Hint: Keep your treats/toys (and clicker/trick props if required) next to the kettle, you can use your tea/coffee breaks to train your dog. Each time you boil the kettle begin your session, and once it has boiled you can stop your session - always end on a positive note!

Social Time

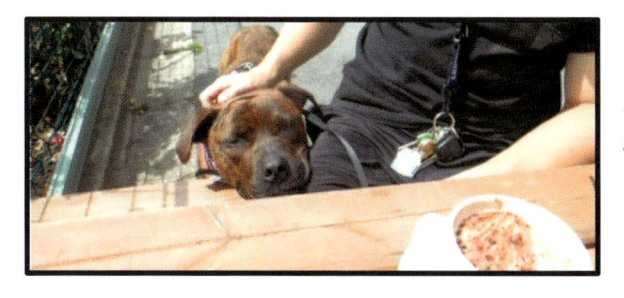

Bosun absolutely loves going to the pub and local cafe!

We walk our dogs for exercise, a change of scenery, to go to the toilet and to socialise with others - although not necessarily other dogs or physical interactions. Rather than thinking of a walk as being a mission to get from A to B or around the block, think about what other options are open to you and your dog and what he/she might wish to do instead. Provided the area is safe, disused or out of hours industrial sites are a sniff-haven for many dogs and are often overlooked.

Charlie going for a coffee with his owner Hayley

Lots of pubs are dog friendly, particularly in their bar area and gardens. Take your dog to have a nice pub lunch or have a catch up coffee with a friend at a dog friendly cafe.

Puppies Bella & Coco enjoying their weekly visit to the local garden centre

Garden centres are often dog friendly too, and some even have a nice cafe too! There are lots of new sights and smells in a garden centre, so have a walk around first and let your dog explore before settling down for a cuppa!

Does your dog have a favourite person who they don't get to see very often? Arranging for them to pop over or to go for a walk together could be really enjoyable for both you and your dog. It is important that we trust who is interacting with our dogs, so a close friend, relative or neighbour could be the perfect person to brighten your dog's day!

Jasper enjoying gentle fuss from his favourite visiting relatives

If your dog has existing dog friends, you can invite them over for a social session in your garden, or hire a local fully enclosed field for playtime with those friends. This can be 1-1 or with a couple of dogs if you and your dog know them all well.

Marcus (darker Golden Retriever) having a playdate with his friends Chief, Barney & Charlie

There are of course individuals who are not sociable with any other dog, animal or person other than their owners. If you do have a dog who does not feel comfortable in the presence of other dogs and people, consult a force-free behaviourist to help find a technique that allows your dog to relax and socialise at a distance they are happy with, so they too can enjoy social time within their comfort zone.

Ginny visiting the cows on her walk

Puppy Iyla settling on her mat in a friends garden

HH Hint: Teaching your dog how to settle on a blanket during your mini training sessions can be very beneficial as you can take the blanket to new locations and build up the 'settle down' behaviour around distractions. The more relaxed and well behaved your dog is in new environments, the more likely you are to take them with you!

Amber & Simba settling on their beds at Nan's house

Car Journeys

Going for a car journey can be really enjoyable for dogs, particularly those who can not exercise for long periods of time due to injury, illness, behavioural issues or old age.

D'fer loves a journey in the van - harnessed and clipped in for his safety

Going for car journeys through your local woods, deer park, and places where you can drive slowly can be really mentally stimulating for your dog.

Bobby loves riding up front - harnessed and clipped in for his safety

Alfie & Gillie enjoy the spacious boot where they can watch the world go by

You can combine both 'Social Time' and 'Car Journeys' by taking your dog with you when you go to collect a friend or relative in the car. Always make sure both yourself and the dog are safe whilst the vehicle is moving.

Teach your puppy how to relax in a car from as young as possible, this makes for much more enjoyable car journeys as they grow up.

Start off slowly with just the engine running whilst the car is safely parked on the driveway, give your puppy a Kong or long lasting chew, and sit with them until they have finished.

Puppy Mackeson relaxing in his daily car journey

Older dogs can be taught how to relax in the car too, even if they are already excitable, it just takes a little longer. You can use your mini training sessions to work on this!

Rex - ensuring your dog can be calm in the car before travelling is important

HH Hint: For some dogs a car journey can be too exciting and may cause frustration if there isn't a walk when they arrive at their destination. If this sounds like your dog, or if your dog is frightened of the car, practise little journeys with a stuffed Kong to help teach them a new association of the car first.

Massages

Massages can benefit dogs in many ways. By giving your dog a massage you could improve their blood circulation, increase their oxygenation and release muscle tension, not to mention the relationship bonding between you and your dog during the massage.

Bella loves stopping to have a relaxing massage in the woods

Massages can be used at home as a relaxation technique, or they can be given outside on a walk as a form of enrichment and social bonding. Allow your dog to guide you by massaging the part of their body they choose to give you.

It is difficult for a dog to tell us or show us where tension is hiding in their body, particularly if it's in their back or neck. Relieving tension and pain can massively improve a dog's quality of life.

Busby

Always offer your dog the choice to participate in having a massage, sit on the floor away from your dog and ask them to come into your space instead of you invading their space. Using a mat on the floor allows clear choices to be made, if your dog is on the mat they are happy to continue with the massage, if they get up and move away, they are finished. Respect their choice at all times.

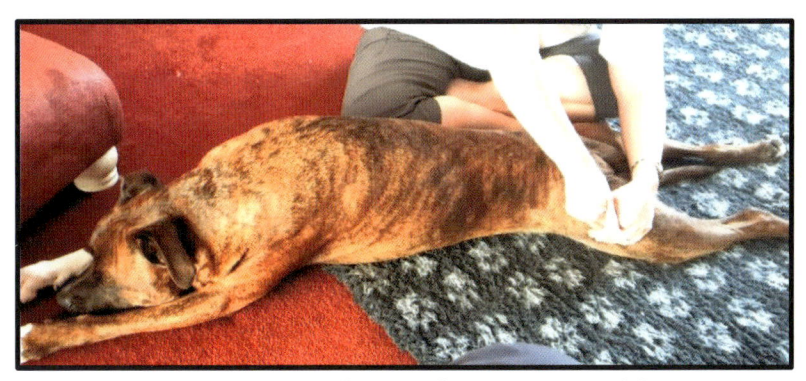

*Bosun stretching out for a massage with his
Clinical Canine Massage Therapist Jenny*

Bosun relaxing into a massage

Clinical Canine Massage is a non-invasive therapy that typically improves a dog's mobility and aims to return them to their normal activities & behaviour. A Guild Therapist utilises a variety of techniques to restore the muscles and fascia throughout the body.

The Canine Massage Guild is a network of highly skilled therapists across the UK who specialise in the Lenton Method. This results-driven approach helps dogs with:

1. soft tissue injury rehabilitation & prevention
2. chronic pain management
3. orthopaedic conditions
4. Maintaining their mobility
5. Anxiety issues
6. Maintaining their condition for sporting performance

Guild Therapists aim to see an improvement in your dog within only 3 sessions and always work with your vet. You can find your local Canine Massage Guild therapist
http://www.k9-massageguild.co.uk/therapistregister/

Free Work

ACE Free Work, developed by Sarah Fisher at Animal Centred Education (ACE) is invaluable for building confidence in dogs whilst providing a blend of stimulation experiences.

An example of a Free Work Setup

Try to vary the textures, heights, smells and how your dog has to interact with each item in order to get the food. For example you can spread pate, cream cheese or peanut butter onto Licky Mats or surfaces, you can use a variety of dry food, fresh meat, vegetables or dried/dehydrated treats and you can hide treats in rolled up towels or blankets, or underneath items.

Pepper deciding where to begin

Include items which are familiar to your dog, which already have your dog's scent on them, such as their mental stimulation toys. Keep watch to see if your dog has a preference. Provide at least one bowl of water for your dog in the area too.

Jack enjoying a good nose and brain workout

When your dog is exploring the items take note of which direction they move in, and if they prefer to eat from the raised items first as this could indicate discomfort in the dogs' neck or spine. Using raised stations can be beneficial for older dogs or those with injuries, so bear this in mind when setting up your Free Work fun.

Dotty loves the added height variations of her Free Work

You can use items from your house and garage that you already have available to you. Alternatively, check out your local thrift shop to add more variety to your Free Work.

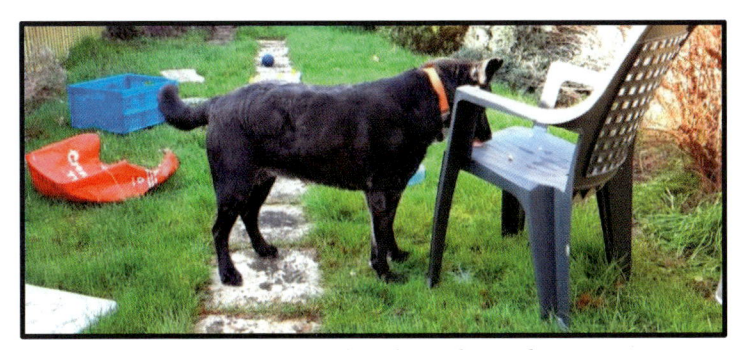

Ginny enjoying Free Work with garden and garage items

HH Hint: Set up the Free Work and place all of the food/spreads/treats out before your dog enters the area. Otherwise you might end up with a dog just following you around to eat every treat as soon as you place it down!

Grooming & Handling

Many dogs are very unhappy and uncomfortable with claw clipping, brushing, teeth checking, putting ear drops in and body checks. This is usually because it is suddenly thrust upon them, and the dog often has no say in whether they'd like to have their fur brushed or their claws clipped.

Bruno learning how to hold a "chin rest" for veterinary examinations

Teaching your dog how to enjoy grooming and handling can seem like a daunting task for some, but it's a fantastic use of time and great for building strong trust between you.

'The Bucket Game' created by Chirag Patel is a popular way to introduce choice based handling/grooming sessions.

Amber practising a "chin rest" as the start of her ear drops training

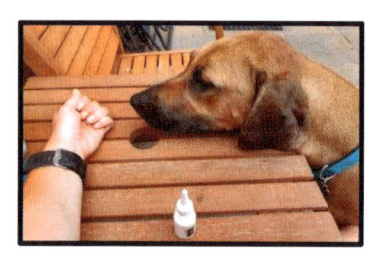

Holly choosing to lay on her mat to participate in a "nail maintenance" session

Always ensure your dog is fully aware that a grooming or handling session is about to begin. Place a mat on the floor for your dog to sit or lay on to symbolise their want to participate. If at any time your dog pulls away or moves away from you and the mat, accept this form of communication.

Allow your dog to move away, as it is important they know that they can end the session at any time. Keep your mat for grooming and handling training only, put it away out of sight when you are not using it. Smaller dogs can be taught how to climb onto a higher surface to participate in their handling & grooming sessions, this will ensure you are not leaning over them too much which can seem intimidating. Always allow the choice for your dog to move away or climb down from their grooming station.

Riv learning to "stand tall" on a surface and hold her position for tummy checks

Work on something that your dog is good at and is happy to participate in before moving onto anything that they are not currently comfortable with. Gentle stroking with the back of your hand may be a good starting point.

It is necessary for some dogs to wear a muzzle. This is also something that should be taught slowly with choice based training and lots of rewards! Not only is Muzzle Desensitising a fun game to play, but it also might be needed one day and your dog will be very grateful for the existing positive association.

Pippa playing Muzzle Games with a plastic cone in our Growly Dog Class

Holding the muzzle in between your legs instead of in your hand ensures your dog is fully in control of putting their face in and out of the muzzle.

Jack practising his "muzzle desensitising" training

Praise and reward your dog when they look or sniff at the muzzle, keep building up rewarding your dog for interacting with the muzzle until they are comfortable enough to put their nose inside. Then you can work on building up duration before praising and rewarding.

HH Hint: Take the time to desensitise dogs to anything they may be wearing, including collars, harnesses, head collars, coats, and even buster collars (from the vets).

Dax loves his muzzle desensitisng sessions

Recycling

There is nothing better than free enrichment for your dog! Keep hold of all of your cardboard boxes, kitchen roll tubes, toilet roll tubes, egg boxes and scrunched up newspaper to create your own unique fun for your dog.

Amber investigating toilet roll tubes (stuffed with treats) on a string

You're only going to throw it all in the bin anyway, so why not allow your dog to help you shred your recyclables to be even smaller!

Keep hold of larger cardboard boxes too - they can have multiple uses from hiding treats in between balls/toys to creating mazes, or even just for keeping all of your other recyclable items in!

Fold one end of the tubes and fill them with a few treats before folding the opposite end

Egg boxes also make great slow feeders for dinner time

Bella & Coco enjoy snuffling for treats inside their ball filled cardboard box

Busby loves to find treats from a large box with shredded cardboard inside

Mass destruction is great fun, and is another naturally occurring behaviour for dogs! It's much better if your dog enjoys shredding and ripping apart recyclable items than some of your more valuable ones!

Pepper shredding an egg box

HH Hint: Choose cardboard items over plastic items as some plastic can be quite sharp (and noisy!!) when chewed on. Ask neighbours, friends and relatives to save up their recyclable items for your dog too!

Thank you for reading, I really hope that you've enjoyed this little book, and it has given you some ideas to introduce to your dogs' daily routine.

I am so very lucky to have a wonderful job, working with many lovely dogs and their owners. Mental stimulation is such a fun and valuable part of my job and I am so delighted to share photos of our furry family with you. I loved every minute of searching through all of my dog photos to find the perfect ones for this book.

If you find the time please consider leaving a review on Amazon for other dog lovers to read. Reviews dictate the continuing success of self-published authors.

Many thanks

Ellie x

Useful Links

Haines Hounds Dog Training
www.haineshounds.com

Haines Hounds Dog Training on FB
www.facebook.com/HainesHoundsDogTraining

Blue Cross Muzzle Training
www.bluecross.org.uk/pet-advice/dogs-and-muzzle-training

Canine Massage Therapy Centre
www.k9-massage.co.uk

Canine Massage Therapist, Jenny Youdan
http://www.k9elements.co.uk/

Canine Enrichment and Training on FB
www.facebook.com/groups/1036238453218381

Chirag Patel's 'The Bucket Game' on FB
www.facebook.com/thebucketgame

Chirag Patel's 'The Counting Game'
https://clickerexpo.clickertraining.com/the-counting-game/

Nail Maintenance For Dogs on FB
www.facebook.com/groups/nail.maintenance.for.dogs

Animal Behaviour & Training Council (ABTC) www.abtcouncil.org.uk

Animal Centred Education (ACE) www.tilleyfarm.org.uk/AceIndex.php

Association of Pet Dog Trainers (APDT UK) www.apdt.co.uk

Institute of Modern Dog Trainers (IMDT) www.imdt.uk.com

Recommended Reading

Beverley Courtney (2017) *Calm Down!:* Step-by-Step to a Calm, Relaxed, and Brilliant Family Dog (Essential Skills for a Brilliant Family Dog), Independently Published.

Grisha Stewart (2016) *Behavior Adjustment Training 2.0:* New Practical Techniques for Fear, Frustration, and Aggression in Dogs, Dogwise Publishing.

Janet Finlay (2019) *Your End of the Lead:* Changing how you think and act to help your reactive dog, Independently Published.

Linda Tellington-Jones (2013) *Getting in TTouch with Your Dog:* A Gentle Approach to Influencing Behaviour, Health and Performance, Quiller Publishing Ltd.

Rosie Lowry (2017) *Understanding The Silent Communication Of Dogs*, Lowry Industries Ltd; 2nd Revised edition (13 July 2017).

Sarah Fisher (2007) *Unlock Your Dog's Potential:* How to Achieve a Calm and Happy Canine, David & Charles.

Sarah Whitehead (2013) *Clever Dog:* Understand What Your Dog Is Telling You, HarperCollins Publishers.

Steve Mann (2019) *Easy Peasy Puppy Squeezy:* Your simple step-by-step guide to raising and training a happy puppy or dog, Blink Publishing.

Printed in Great Britain
by Amazon